PETS PLUS

Dogs

Sally Morgan

A+

Smart Apple Media

Published by Smart Apple Media, an imprint of Black Rabbit Books
P.O. Box 3263, Mankato, Minnesota 56002
www.blackrabbitbooks.com

Printed in the United States of America at Corporate Graphics, Inc. North Mankato, Minnesota.

Published by arrangement with the Watts Publishing Group LTD, London.

Library of Congress Cataloging-in-Publication Data
 Morgan, Sally, 1957-
  Dogs / Sally Morgan.
    p. cm. -- (Pets plus)
  Includes index.
  Summary: "Describes behavioral characteristics of wild and domestic dogs. Helps readers decide if a pet dog is right for them, and gives suggestions on caring for a pet dog"--Provided by publisher.
  ISBN 978-1-59920-699-8 (library binding)
 1. Dogs--Juvenile literature. 2. Dogs--Behavior--Juvenile literature.
 3. Wild dogs--Juvenile literature. I. Title.
 SF426.5.M65 2012
 636.7--dc23
                        2011024871

Created by Taglines Creative Ltd: www.taglinescreative.com
Author: Sally Morgan
Series designer: Hayley Cove
Editor: Jean Coppendale

Picture credits
t=top b=bottom l=left r=right m=middle
Cover: Dog Shutterstock/Eric Isselee; Wolf Shutterstock/Holly Kuchera; PP fur Shutterstock/Big Pants Production; beagle Shutterstock/ Eri Isselee. p4l Ecoscene/Pete Cairns; 4r Shutterstock/Sergey Skleznev; p5 Ecoscene/Chinch Gryniewicz; p6 Shutterstock/Sonya Etchison; p7t Shutterstock/Bailey One, 7b Shutterstock/Monkey Business; p8 Kevin Wiltshire; p9 Shutterstock/Annette Shaff, 9b Shutterstock Karen Roach (lead), Raymond Kasprzak (ball), Jiri Pavlik (dumbbell); p10 &11 Ecoscene/Angela Hampton; p12 Ardea/Jean Paul Ferrero; p13 & 14 Ecoscene/Angela Hampton; p15 Shutterstock/Sonya Etchison; p16l Shutterstock/Francesca Miller, 16r Tonis Valing; p17 Shutterstock/Boris Djuranovic; p18 Ardea/M Watson; p19 top left to right Shutterstock /Svetlana Valoueva, Sbolotova, Steam Roller Blues, 19b Shutterstock /Vahamrick; p20l/r Shutterstock/Wolf Mountain, Ales Nowak; p21 Shutterstock/fdenb; p22t Ecoscene/Angela Hampton, 22b Alamy/Michael Sewell; p23t Ecoscene/Fritz Polking, 23b Ecoscene/Angela Hampton; p24t Ecoscene/ Angela Hampton, 24b Ecoscene/Steve Kazlowski; p25 Shutterstock/ Ewan Chessar; p26 Shutterstock/Pixshots; p27 Ardea/Jean-Paul Ferrero; p29 Ecoscene /Angela Hampton; p32 Shutterstock/Aneta Pics;

PO 1562 / Nov 2012

9 8 7 6 5 4 3 2

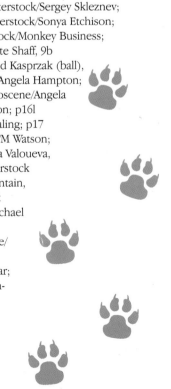

Contents

The meaning of the words in **bold** can be found in the glossary on pages 30–31.

Pet Dogs, Wild Dogs

Dogs have lived with humans for thousands of years, but they still have lots in common with their wild cousins.

Wild Dogs

The friendly pet dog is **descended** from the wolf and is related to wild dogs, such as dingoes found in Australia, African hunting dogs, and the **dhole** and raccoon dogs in Asia. Some pet dogs look like the wolf; the husky for example, with its thick coat and broad head.

▼ The wolf (left) and husky (right) look very similar with erect ears, fur around the face, and a pointed **muzzle**.

▲ Some collie dogs are working dogs used by farmers to herd and look after their sheep.

Man's Best Friend

Dogs have lived with people for at least 15,000 years, and possibly for as long as 100,000 years. Dogs were found around the first settlements where they fed on scraps of food left by people, a bit like coyotes in towns and cities today. Gradually, the dogs became **tame** and people took them into their homes.

Jobs for Dogs

People started to breed dogs to do a particular job. Larger dogs were used to guard people and animals, collie-like dogs herded animals. Dogs that had a good sense of smell were used for hunting. In the snowy Arctic, huskies are still used to pull sleds.

PET POINT

A dog that is a particular breed is called a pedigree dog. A mixed breed is a cross between different breeds.

Why a Dog?

Dogs are great pets. They are animals that love to live with people and they can help to keep you fit.

Things to Think About

Dogs make great friends but they need a lot of looking after.

POINTS IN FAVOR OF HAVING A DOG

- companionship; you are never alone when you own a dog
- dogs love to be cuddled and to play with you
- dogs help to keep you fit

POINTS TO THINK ABOUT BEFORE GETTING A DOG

- you need plenty of spare time
- dogs need training
- dogs need a walk every day, even in bad weather
- dogs cannot be left on their own for many hours
- all dogs, but especially long haired dogs, need daily brushing
- vet's bills can be expensive

◀ Going out for a run with your dog is a fun way to exercise for both of you.

▶ This miniature schnauzer is a pedigree dog.

Pedigree or Mixed Breed?

Many people choose to buy a pedigree dog because they are **purebred** and they like the look or character of the breed. Pedigree dogs are usually bought from **breeders** and these dogs can be very expensive. A mixed breed is cheaper, but when you buy a mixed breed puppy, you can never be sure of how large it will grow and what it will be like when it's older.

▼ An animal shelter will often have pedigree as well as mixed breed dogs that need a home.

Rescue Dogs

Many people now get puppies and adult dogs from **animal shelters** where there are unwanted or stray dogs looking for new homes. People give up their pet for many reasons, for example they may be moving away, can't afford the dog anymore, or they are too sick to look after it.

PET POINT
Animal shelters are very careful to match you to the right type of dog for your family.

Your Pet's New Home

Bringing home a new dog is very exciting for you, but it can be a very stressful time for your new pet whether it is a puppy or an adult dog.

Getting Ready

Make sure you have everything you need to look after your new pet before you bring it home. A dog needs a bed and some bedding. You will need dog food, so ask the breeder or the animal shelter what food you should buy.

▼ Put your dog's bed in a quiet, warm place where it can sleep and not be disturbed.

Exploring

Let your new pet explore. Try to be quiet and don't play with it too much. It may be scared and not sure where to go. Show it where to find its bed and water bowl. Make sure there are no wires for your pet to trip over or chew on. Any dangerous objects, such as prickly plants or sharp ornaments, should be put out of reach of your pet.

Other Pets

If you already have a pet, make sure someone is always in the room with them until they get used to each other. But don't ignore your other pet and spend all your time with the new dog.

▲ Not all pets will get along as well as these two, so keep an eye on them.

PET POINT
Puppies often cry in the night because they feel lonely. A loud ticking clock near their bed may help to make them feel more secure.

Potty Training

If you have a puppy, it's very important to start potty training as soon as you get it home. Take it outside after every meal and as soon as it wakes up in the morning. Stay with it until it has peed or pooped. It will soon learn what you want it to do.

Do It!

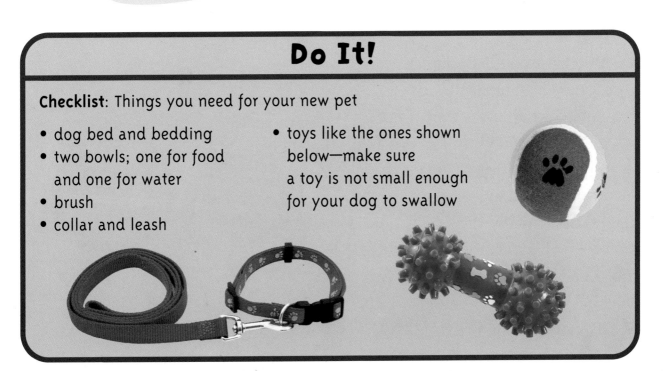

Checklist: Things you need for your new pet

- dog bed and bedding
- two bowls; one for food and one for water
- brush
- collar and leash
- toys like the ones shown below—make sure a toy is not small enough for your dog to swallow

Caring for Your Dog

There is a lot to remember when you keep a dog. It needs regular meals, fresh water, grooming, and exercise.

Feeding Your Pet

A puppy has three or four small meals each day. As it gets older it needs two larger meals a day instead. The breeder or animal shelter will tell you the right way to feed your dog. Try not to feed it too much. Dogs can get overweight just like people, and it's not good for them.

Walks

An adult dog needs plenty of exercise to stay healthy. Most dogs need to go for a walk twice a day so they can run around and explore. Puppies do not need much exercise for the first few months as they are still growing. You should never exercise a dog before or just after its meal as this can make it sick.

▲ Your pet should always have a bowl of clean water to drink.

Grooming

All dogs, even those with short hair, should be brushed once a day. Dogs with very long coats will need longer and more regular brushing. Always brush a dog's coat in the direction the hair is growing. In the wild, wolves groom their own fur to keep it clean. Sometimes one wolf grooms another.

Do It!

Plan a routine for when you will feed, walk, and brush your pet. It is best to feed your pet at about the same time each day.

▼ All dogs need to be brushed regularly to stop their hair from becoming dirty and tangled.

Wild Cousins

The dog's closest relative is the gray wolf, a feared hunter that once lived across much of the **Northern Hemisphere**.

Living in a Pack

Wolves live in groups called **packs**. A pack usually consists of between 8 and 15 animals. Each pack lives in an area called a **territory**, which they guard from other packs. The pack is led by the top male and female dogs. These are usually the oldest wolves with the most experience. They often lead the pack on the hunt for food.

Pouncing

A single wolf will hunt small prey, such as mice, hares, and birds. It listens for the animal moving in the undergrowth and then pounces with its front paws. Pet dogs also do this. They stand still with their head tilted to one side listening for the squeaks of a small animal.

▼ Wolves hunt in a pack and kill large animals such as caribou, moose, deer, and sheep.

▲ Pet dogs are using their "wild" hunting skills when they play games such as chasing a ball.

Chasing Prey

The urge to chase prey can be seen in many dogs. Pet dogs may chase squirrels and rabbits and unfortunately, some chase and kill farm animals. Even well-trained dogs should be kept on a leash if you are near other animals. Sometimes their **instinct** to chase prey is too strong to control.

Do It!

Play games with your dog, such as chasing balls and other toys. If you throw a stick, make sure it does not have any sharp points that might scratch or cut your dog's mouth. You should not throw stones or rocks for your dog.

Training Your Dog

Dogs need to be trained if they are to grow into **obedient**, well-behaved pets. They are intelligent animals and learn quickly.

Pack Order

In a wolf pack, the top wolf controls the behavior of the rest of the pack. It's the same with your pet. It will think of you as the "top dog" and it will want to please you.

Sit and Stay

It is easy to teach your pet basic commands, such as sit, stay, and come, using small treats as rewards. Say the word "sit" and push gently on its bottom to make it sit. Then give it a treat. When you are training your pet, speak clearly and firmly.

▲ Your pet will soon learn that when it sits, it gets a tasty reward.

Calling Your Pet

When you go outside with your pet, make it walk beside you. Say the command "heel" and pull the dog back if it gets ahead of you. Reward it with a treat when it is walking at heel. Before you let your dog off the leash outdoors, you must be sure it will come to you when you call its name. Whenever you talk to your pet use its name. Train it to sit and then come to you when you call it.

▲ When you walk along a path, keep your dog close on one side.

Be Gentle

Don't get angry with your dog when it is naughty. Be gentle and calm and never, ever hit your dog. Make sure everybody in your family uses the same command words so the dog does not get confused by different words.

Working Dogs

Over thousands of years, people have **bred** dogs to work. Dogs guard, hunt, and even care for people.

Hunting Dogs

Wolves and wild dogs have an excellent sense of smell that they use to find food in the wild. Many pet dogs also have a very good sense of smell. Some dogs are used by people for hunting birds and deer. Dogs can also be trained to follow human scent and are used by the police to catch criminals on the run. Other dogs are trained to sniff out drugs and explosives.

Guard Dogs

In the past, dogs such as German shepherds were used to protect sheep from wolves and other **predators**. Now, they are often used to guard property.

▲ Some owners train their pet to guard the house.

◀ Police dogs are trained to sniff out drugs and bombs.

Service Dogs

Some dogs can be trained to help people with disabilities. Guide dogs live with people who are blind or partially sighted. The dogs are trained to guide their owners along streets and across roads. Hearing dogs help people with hearing disabilities. They will let their owner know when the doorbell is ringing or if something is wrong.

Visiting Dogs

Doctors have found that stroking or patting a pet such as a dog can help sick people to feel better. There are special groups that organize pet visits. People take their pet dogs to hospitals and **nursing homes** to visit the sick and elderly. The dogs have to be quiet and friendly and enjoy being petted a lot.

▲ Guide dogs are picked when they are puppies and given special training.

cubs and Pups

A female wolf gives birth to a **litter** of young called cubs. The young of a dog are called puppies.

Wolves and Cubs

A female wolf mates in February or March and gives birth to her cubs abouth two months later. The cubs are born somewhere warm and safe, such as a cave. The cubs stay here for about three weeks and then they will join the pack.

At first the cubs feed on their mother's milk, but once they are four weeks old, they start to eat meat.

▼ These wolf cubs touch their mother's mouth to ask for food. The mother brings up food from her stomach for the cubs to eat.

Life Cycle

A female wolf breeds when she is about two to three years of age. Wild and pet dogs, like the husky shown here, feed their young milk for the first few weeks. Pet dogs are old enough to leave their mother when they are about eight weeks old. Some wild dogs and wolves remain in the pack for life, but others move away to start their own pack.

3-week old pups

8-week old puppy

young adult

▼ Like the wolf cubs, these puppies nuzzle their mother asking for food.

Dogs and Puppies

A female dog can be mated twice a year at any time. She is pregnant for about two months, just like a female wolf. However, female dogs give birth to larger litters than a wolf, usually between 5 and 10 puppies. Like a wolf, a pet dog looks for a quiet place in which to give birth.

Growing Up

Cubs and puppies have a lot to learn as they are growing up. They do this through their play.

Play Fighting

Wolf cubs like to roll around with each other and play fight. This helps them to learn skills that they will need as adults when they hunt for food. When puppies are about five to six weeks old, they also play a lot. Through play they learn about each other and one pup will usually come out on top. This will be the top dog who is first to the food and first out of the door!

▼ Cubs (left) and pups (right) roll and tumble together and soon find out who is top wolf and top dog.

▲ Make sure your pet has a toy it can chew, such as a plastic ball or a tough nylon bone.

Don't Bite!

Young pups and cubs bite each other as they play. This is all part of growing up. In the wild, young wolf cubs get scolded with a nip if they bite the adults or other cubs too hard. Young pups need to be taught not to bite, too. If your pup's teeth make contact with your skin, cry out "ouch" and say "no," so that it learns that you do not like it.

The Right Bite

To help strengthen your pet's teeth and jaws, give your pet strong toys it can bite and chew. Play tug of war with "tug" toys you can buy from pet shops—but don't get too rough.

Do It!

In the wild, wolves learn to use their nose to find animals hiding in the undergrowth. This hide-and-seek game will help your puppy to develop its hunting skills. Make your puppy sit and stay. Then hide and call it to you. If it finds you easily, try hiding farther away.

Your Wild Pet

If you watch your pet, you may see that it does many things that wolves, dingoes, and other wild dogs do in the wild.

Marking

Male dogs like to pee on lampposts and fences. Other dogs pick up the smell of the **urine** which acts like a note saying "I was here." For wolves in the wild this marking is very important. Males mark the edges of their territory by peeing on tree trunks and rocks. Wolves in other packs smell the urine and stay away.

▼ Wolves mark their territory and so do pet dogs. Male dogs start to lift their leg when they are about eight to nine months old.

Rolling Over

When a wolf in a pack rolls over on its side to show its belly to another wolf, this is a sign that it is no threat to the other wolf. Pet dogs do this, too. Sometimes when two dogs meet, one dog will lie down in front of the other dog to show it is not a threat.

▲ Both wild dogs, such as the African hunting dogs (top), and pet dogs (below) quickly find out who's boss.

Dog Talk

The howl of a wolf and the bark of a dog are both important means of communication, but dogs also communicate in other ways.

Barks and Growls

When a wolf howls, this is a way of telling other wolves that it is around. Dogs do not howl, they bark instead. They bark to tell their owners about strangers who may be approaching, or that something is wrong. Dogs also growl. This is a warning that they are not happy and that they may bite.

▼ Pet dogs and wolves may bare their teeth or mouth at each other to see who is top dog, but they do not bite.

Stay Away

A wolf that is about to attack another curls its lips back to show off its teeth, stares at the other wolf, and raises the hairs on its neck and back to look larger. When two wolves have a "stare-off," one may turn its head away, look at the ground, and lower its tail to avoid a fight. Some male pet dogs do the same when they meet.

Wagging Tails

Dogs also use their tails to communicate. They wag their tails when they are happy, and tuck their tail under their body if they are scared, unhappy, or not well. Pet dogs get excited when their owners return, and the same happens with wild dogs. When a member of the pack returns, they are greeted with wagging tails.

▲ These African hunting dogs are sniffing each other and wagging their tails in greeting.

Instant Expert

The dog, wolf, and dingo have the Latin name *Canis lupus*. Their closest relatives include the African wild dog, jackals, and foxes.

Large...

The largest wolves are the gray wolves of the Arctic. The males are about 6.5 ft. (2 m) long (nose to tail), stand about 30 in. (76 cm) at the shoulder, and weigh up to 176 lb. (80 kg). The females are smaller.

The heaviest breeds of dog are the St. Bernard and the mastiff. These large dogs weigh up to 258 lb. (117 kg) and stand about 28 in. (72 cm) at the shoulder. The tallest breeds are the Great Dane and Irish wolfhounds that stand about 32–34 in. (82–87 cm) high at the shoulder.

...and Small

The smallest wolf is the Arabian wolf of the Middle East. This desert wolf lives in small groups or pairs rather than large packs and it cannot howl. It weighs about 40 lb. (18 kg) and stands 26 in. (66 cm) high at the shoulder.

The smallest breed of dog is the chihuahua that stands just 6–9 in. (15–23 cm) at the shoulder and weighs between 3–6 lb. (1.3–2.7 kg).

▶ This Great Dane towers over the tiny chihuahua.

Hunting Together

Wolves kill large animals such as caribou and deer. This is possible because the pack hunts together. For example, when the pack chases a herd of caribou, the older and weaker animals get separated and are easier for the wolves to catch. When they are hunting, a pack of wolves can cover a vast distance each day, sometimes as much as 60 miles (96 km) or more.

Life Lines

Wolves have a life span of 6 to 7 years in the wild, and 16 years in captivity. A pet dog lives on average between 10 and 12 years. Smaller dogs usually live longer than the giant breeds.

FAST FACT
Wolves and dogs have 42 teeth including four long canines that they use to grip their food.

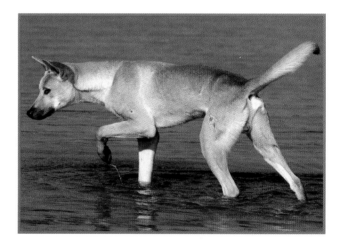

▲ Dingoes are the size of a medium dog with a broad head and pointed snout.

Dingoes

Dingoes are wild dogs that are found in Australia. Their coat is orange-brown in color, often with white marks. They howl like wolves and rarely bark. Like wolves, they are predators and feed on kangaroos, wallabies, birds, and insects.

FAST FACT
Wolves and dogs lick their wounds because their saliva contains substances that speed up healing.

Pet Quiz

Now that you know a bit more about what is involved in looking after dogs, is a dog the right pet for you?

1. **How much time do you have to look after a pet?**
- **a)** Lots of time before and after school and on weekends
- **b)** Not much—I'm very busy with clubs and my friends
- **c)** About an hour a day

2. **Is it important that you play with your pet?**
- **a)** Yes, very important
- **b)** I can play when I'm not doing anything else
- **c)** It might get boring

3. **Does your home have a yard?**
- **a)** Yes, we have a large yard
- **b)** There is a small yard
- **c)** There is no yard

4. **Are you prepared to walk your dog twice a day?**
- **a)** Yes, I love being outside
- **b)** If it's sunny, but not if it's raining
- **c)** I hate walking

5. **Is there somebody at home during the day to look after the dog?**
- **a)** Yes, my parent/guardian is at home all day
- **b)** There is somebody at home for part of the day
- **c)** There is nobody at home during the day

Pet Quiz - Results

If you answered **(a)** to most of the questions then a dog could be for you.

Owning a Pet: Checklist

All pets need to be treated with respect. Always remember your pet can feel pain and distress. It is not a toy.

To be a good pet owner you should try to remember these five rules. Your pet must:

- never suffer from fear and distress
- never be left hungry or thirsty
- never suffer discomfort
- be free from pain, injury, and disease
- have the freedom to show its normal behavior

This means that you have to check your pet every day to make sure it has enough water and food. You must remember to buy new supplies of its food in plenty of time so that it never goes hungry.

You must make sure it has plenty of exercise and is taken for walks— even in the rain or the snow.

You must never hurt your pet, shout at it, scare it, or leave it on its own for long periods of time. If it is sick or hurts itself, you must take it to a vet.

Microchipping

The best way to make sure your dog never gets lost is to microchip it. A microchip is a tiny object, the size of a grain of rice, that is inserted under the skin. To identify the dog, a special scanner is passed over the chip to get a number which is linked to your address.

Glossary

animal shelters places where stray, unwanted, and injured animals can be taken and cared for

bred when dogs are mated to make a puppy with certain features

breed a particular type of dog, such as the dalmatian below

breeders people who keep animals, such as dogs, to breed and sell

descended to come from the same family; to have features passed from one generation to the next, for example from dog to puppy

dhole a type of wild dog found in Asia

instinct natural ability that an animal is born with and does not have to learn

litter a group of cubs or puppies born at the same time

mixed breed a dog that is not purebred but has mixed parentage from two or more different breeds

muzzle the part of the head of a dog that sticks out and includes the nose, mouth and jaws; it may also be called a snout.

Northern Hemisphere the half of the Earth that lies north of the Equator

nursing homes places where sick and elderly people are cared for

obedient well-behaved and doing as they are told

pack a group of wolves or wild dogs that live together

pedigree a purebred dog whose ancestry can be traced

predator an animal, such as the wolf, that hunts other animals for food

purebred an animal that belongs to a particular breed, for example, a cocker spaniel

saliva the liquid in the mouth that makes it easier to swallow food and helps digestion

tame to become used to being with people

territory a particular place or area where an animal or group of animals lives

urine liquid waste that is produced by the kidneys

Websites

Read some tips on training and overcoming problems with your pet dog from PBS's series _Woof_!
http://www.pbs.org/wgbh/woof/index.html

Learn about a few different dog breeds.
http://www.loveyourdog.com/breeds.html

Learn more about working dogs and how they help the FBI.
http://www.fbi.gov/fun-games/kids/kids-dogs

Find a shelter where you can adopt rescue dogs!
http://www.animalshelter.org

Index